fukushima
fortune cookies

BOOKS BY HUNTER REYNOLDS

Brave New Prayers

The 12 Wheels of Karma

FUKUSHIMA

fortune cookies

Hunter
Reynolds

flaming seed
press

978-0-9892605-2-7

Book design: Jane Brunette

Cover photo and interior artwork used with permission of Istock.

Printed in the United States of America.

Published by flamingseed press
flamingseedpress.com

To my beloved teacher, Mooji—
the lion in my path.

contents

Part 1:
Intelligent Groaning

Part 2:

This Howling Moment

Part 3:
Win Yourself Back

I

intelligent groaning

Fukushima Fortune Cookies

Cookie #1
Geiger yourself constantly
for unsafe levels of doom.

Cookie #2
You've been channel surfing
between trite and tragic your whole life.
Less desperate times would solve nothing.

Cookie #3
What are the leaking fuel rods
that shorten the lifespan of compassion?

Cookie #4
Red rash of opinion or stigmata of presence:
The fissioning skull contaminates everyone.

Cookie #5
Uranium lava needs containment
more than ego needs a witness?

Cookie #6
Before speaking: look down.
See ash white femurs poking from shoes
that outlive you.

Cookie #7
No-mind can endure
this kind of humiliation.

Intelligent Groaning

Gunned down, legless,
an explosion of stars
looks down
at civil war stumps.

This is meditation.

Bleeding free
of the tension it takes to exist,
ancient worries
unclench like a fist.

This is meditation.

Thought-wind billowing
the red cross yurt,
chatting up the worried love.
Clear seeing on red alert.

This is meditation.

Smiling
at the medical "ethics"—
lies about the wonders
of modern prosthetics.

This is meditation.

Pretending to lament
the expired allowance of steps,
the intelligent groaning,
the meaningless suspense.

This is meditation.

Night Clerk

Admit it.

You're a seedy hotel—
a crash pad for lonely drifter thoughts, like:
"Marinating in the universal being
is going to make me un-interesting."

And you know exactly why you're depressed.

You shampoo dim, shag carpet hallways religiously
yet a cerebral stench still hangs in the air:
"Abiding as pure awareness
would sterilize all personal intimacy
and turn me into a social misfit."

Saddest of all,
the way your charms—
those lumpy, old lobby chairs
that nobody sits in for long—
pull in wave after wave
of desperate, shivering travelers.

At times like these,
we night clerks have a choice:
keep fluffing up the dusty dinosaurs in the lobby

or quickly, without thinking,
empty all the rooms, up our rates
and start catering to the niche traveler
(timeless presence)
who will pay just about anything to sprawl,
luxuriously retro,
in our stiff, flea-market sheets.

Sky of Anyone

Immortal, yet anxious,
humans don't sense
the grandparent beings
looking through them.
Instead, they stand up taller.
Who, then, is doing the looking?
We know the answer, of course.
But, sadly, our styles of dodging it
have been perfected into an art.

They call that "personality."

Seems angelic old folk
want to rock together
on the front porch
of earth-bound faces
but we would rather take turns
caressing each other's birth certificates.

They call that "sexy."

According to these worship-less
whippersnappers,
the iridescent mandalas that glow
at the bottom of the warm pools

we gaze through
are curious accidents
flushed from the barren belly
we call "space."

Why not fill 'em up
with like and dislike?

Makes you wonder
what kind of traumatic back story
might explain
this kind of callous elder abuse?
Try this:
we grew up watching our parents
(eternity and edges)
go through a nasty divorce
and now we're too proudly orphaned
to fall into the sky
of anyone.

Cave Dwellers

In Paleolithic, pre-tech times
(a few months ago)
before "well-being" got upgraded
into a friendlier format
(standard, dignified anguish)
and the God-eared confessors
backed off
into "life coach" caves
far from the full-spectrum light
that makes screen-saver egos
look anemic white

humans weren't evolved enough
to sleep in tiny, chiseled hollows
called "my purpose."
In those days, falling droplets of ambition,
instead of exploding like fire crackers,
simply kerplunked.

Hard to believe there are still
aggressively un-hunched freaks
roaming the open air—
Humanoids who refuse to sit
bloodshot

around the fluorescent fires,
squinting
through the stinging smoke of time.

No matter.
It's just a matter of time
before our modern witch doctors
round them all up
and bring them up to speed.

It's sad, really,
but somehow inevitable,
to watch our genetic cousins
backing themselves into
an existential corner,
clinging to the Voodoo belief
that the software of the human eye
is the ultimate mobile interface:

a portal to timeless communion
and limitless belonging,
forever immune
to updates.

Cosmic Confession

Engrossed
in my changing self-portrait
Grasping
at a retreating mirage:
beauty, pleasure, power

I have become Robosapien.

I fling belief
like a boozy dart thrower.
Who views
point of view?
I couldn't care less.

Homes grow cold.
Success never satisfies.
Still, I grow fat
in the easy chair
of ambition.

Leadership means
wrestling free of ego
on a public stage.
My attempts to prepare?

An impossibility
that has become
a way of life.

Only a mad
penetrating presence
could catch divinity
playing hide and seek
with itself
in this age
of vacant depression.

Instead
I judge
or join them.

Grease Monkeys

Admit it:
A grease monkey has mounted
your eyelash'd immensity

The whole world is nothing
but a garage full of drunken mechanics
jabbing plugs
into the bald tire of belief.

Yoga bunnies, hot monks
yanking limply
on the frozen bolt of gender.

Nostalgic tinkerers
jerry rigging a joyride
in a vintage self-image.

One has to wonder:
Is anything actually getting repaired down here?

Not much.

At least, not until we confess:
rusting clunkers can't fix
rusting clunkers
and tears are the tune-up
we do best.

Chemtrails

The most compelling thing
about conspiracy theory repartee
is the counterfeit communion
in each dark assertion:
the intimacy of shared aversion.

Tasty, deep-fried
reptilians provide
a chummy kind of suicide.

In fact, the slightest treasonous intonation
does to inner revelation
what Round-up does
to the smooth caramel cheeks
of the indigenous nation.

Admit it.
There's something scarier
than cesium-tainted milk:
refusing to postulate
so positive intention
can bioaccumulate.

The solution?

Irritate
the lungs of aloofness.

Aerosolize
your broken heart.

These are the Chemtrails
that really freak us out.

Gossip

Like wind
calls attention
to space

may gossip
be the breath
of the faceless
face.

Hungry Ghost

Hey hungry ghost
I see you in there
turning the ministry of minutes
into pointless playthings.
That's right, I'm talking to you,
anorexic eyes.
Listen up.

There's a reason
you've read this far:
An imperceptible nightmare
is begging for the relief
of being named.
And so, grim minister
of this godless mess,
I will oblige.

A dark angel
has got your dead-eyed
put-togetherness pride
pinned naked
against an icy dumpster.
I know. It's humiliating.
But remember,
it's not personal.

Your regret-scarred DNA
has simply caught up to you
and "prayer"—
that thing you call
"the psychological equivalent
of biting your fingernails"—
might not be such a bad idea

right now.

Still Want It?

You say you want thought to be dust
under the feet of awareness.
But what if that means
the din of opinion
starts sounding
like a porn star's
commodified moans?

Still want it?

You say you want to catch
Beingness exhaling the world.
But what if that means
feeling weepy with worship
to a god that glows in the eyes
of a "fountain-pen killer"
greedily crumbling
the economies of the world
with a smile?

Still want it?

You say you want to say goodbye
to the mythical "I."
But what if that means

you can't go to the supermarket
without parting, like Moses,
a vast, ethereal sea—
all name and form: just floating debris?

Still want it?

You say you're ready to stop hiding
behind your birth name—
the schizophrenia that divides seer from seen.
But what if that means
each slowly savored blink
becomes an extinction-level event
and smiles from a promising soul mate
feel only slightly more personal
than promotional mail
from a credit card company?

Still want it?

Twilight

Black hand of night
pressed tight together
with bright palm of day:

Transform this twilight,
our hope so slender,
into an endless namaste.

2

this howling
moment

This Howling Moment

Ever wonder
why those swirling cyclones
on the weather channel
get saddled with mortal names?

Perhaps we're hankering
for a prescient metaphor—
hints to help us prepare
for that howling moment
when me-stories,
nailed like plywood
over eyelash'd windows,
pry loose and fly away.

Perhaps, our soul reasons,
if I muddy the line
between dude and disaster,
we'll go for the third option.
Crouch quiet enough
in our heart-basements
and we just might hear something
more dumbfounding
than swing sets, bicycles and spare tires
lifting suddenly
like a flock of birds.

Storm fronts
fondly named
are all we've ever known.

Is not everyone a weather man
glibly tracing
a frightening devastation?
The "Who-I-was-yesterday-ness"
lodged like a refrigerator
in the branches of each face.

Most alarming—
what happens just before
each howling moment
makes landfall:

The eerie stillness
meticulously unsavored.
The bracing, upbeat attitude
as the softly lapping
ocean of tomorrows
recedes
inch-by-ominous-inch.
The static electric chit-chat
desperate for charisma,
crises, porny devices.

The weather we're after?
1-800 rapture.

The Looking

eyeballs looking for their eyeball-ness
the more they aim, the more they miss

silence punching like an empty fist
at the belly of apocalypse

now I know I'm the looking
So aglow with the looking

temple ruins from an ancient war
all the faces we adore

thinky thorns on savior heads
ascended when we go to bed

now I know I'm the looking
so aglow with the looking

warpaint mud on infant cheeks
face of ego when it speaks

plot lines grunting free will dreams
same old actor; different scenes

now I know I'm the looking
so aglow with the looking

Breathy Stranger

I feel you stroking
with planets you call hands.
Such frozen comfort
your Bibles and Korans.

Just like a crime scene
your mysteries only grow.
Lee Harvey Oswald
I am your grassy knoll.

But I'm going to love you anyway—
on the back of my neck
a breathy stranger every day.
I'm going to love you anyway
because I know you're in so close
you're far away.

This boot of flesh
it's too narrow for my toes.
This brain's too baggy
with all the things it knows.

Oh wet religion
religion in each eye.
I love your churches
but your sermons, they're so dry.

But I'm going to love you anyway—
on the back of my neck
a breathy stranger every day.
I'm going to love you anyway
because I know you're in so close
you're far away.

You wave your chainsaw
of silence through each thought.
Big corporation
You clear-cut every lot.

Big limbs are falling.
Quick! Grab a hard hat.
Oh plastic dharma
you're already cracked.

But I'm going to love you anyway—
on the back of my neck
a breathy stranger every day.
I'm going to love you anyway
because I know you're in so close
you're far away.

Just like a miner
black-faced and underground,
this mind keeps digging
not liking what is found.

They say up top
there's a blinding fist of light
that'll deck your dreams
before they get a chance to fight.

But I'm going to love you anyway—
on the back of my neck
a breathy stranger every day.
I'm going to love you anyway
because I know you're in so close
you're far away.

Shackled

Shackled
to the stake of the sky,
attention
yanks and whimpers.

A meaningful life?

Petting
the fevered forehead
of a bloody-ankle'd lamb.

Divine Wikileaks

Captive
inside a hairdo'd embassy,
the ultimate whistle blower:

Supreme Being
caught in a diplomatic deadlock
waiting for safe passage—

the chance to speak freely
on that rare
asylum-granting soil

beneath our feet.

Drone Operator

Porn sites reassuring him
he is anything but machine,
a mild-mannered drone operator
at an underground military base
in Nebraska
jabs suddenly at his keyboard.

Me-stories reassuring us
we are anything but the Unborn,
a violently average ego
at the helm of a dream,
calmly vaporizes
the Witness.

Master Ten-Shun

My Master's name is Ten-Shun.
His teaching style?
Bedtime aches that wake
into spasms,
tissues that won't stop pinching
until I sit through
yet another one of Ten-Shun's
Hellfire sermons:

"Personality" is stylized stress,
charming neuromuscular
sacrilege,
rat poison on the tongue
of every unposed moment
of overflowing
I-don't-knowing.

Pounding on the pre-cancerous Bible
that bears my name,
Master Ten-Shun is
strictly Old Testament,
I-for-an-I:

"Speak always," he scowls,
"as the Imperishable—
so faithfully inflating you
with preverbal baby breaths,
lest the outer I's
become oppressively vivid:
'earnestness freaks' grunting
feelings, needs, and other
beliefist disease."

I once asked Master Ten-Shun why
we should meditate.
His response was delightfully self-deprecating:

"Because we all need a little Ibuprofin
to take the edge off
the chronic throb
of Master Ten-Shun
screaming,
'As what are you speaking?'"

Pink

When moon signs spin
and eyes go dim
and man forgets
whose dream he's in,
rise up great sun
turn grey walls pink,
then take me down
where madmen drown
and mystics drink.

Cyborg Assassin

What can be said
about timeless presence—
this relentless, whining circular saw
at the construction site next door
to everywhere?

I know. You're not used to thinking
of stillness as a metallic assault.

But hasn't this idle hush always been shrill—
a jarring "lack of racket"
made by a pounding deconstruction worker
dead set on autographing the space
between our ears?

I mean, construction workers
eventually stop.
This guy keeps hammering
right on into our dreams.

Perhaps you can sense him,
even now,
dismantling the alert, problem solving
state of consciousness
that's shredding this planet.

Alzheimer's, dementia, mysticism;
One way or another,
he's got a power tool
to help you surrender your head.

But enough of this working-class metaphor.

Could lucid not-knowing be an entity—
a cyborg assassin
sent to us from a dystopian future
to derail
the machine-ification of our species?

When we choose chatting
over meditative relating
are we murdering
the savior of man?

Extinction

Witnessing
the absolute extinction
of every breath,
moment, thought —

fear of endings
subsides.

Purpose?

Kneeling
at the bedside
of now.

Six Names for Saturn

1. Ice Doctor

The icy-hearted god
who pulls the plug
on our ambivalent attachments
so we can grieve our way back
into wholehearted commitment.

2. Incarcerator

The monastic god
who dries up distraction
imprisoning us
in the aloneness we need
to discipline
our squandered talents.

3. Matter Splatter

The infinitely patient god
who never stops stretching
flesh canvases
on which we might splatter
compassion paint
with more abandon.

4. Use-ifer

The socially responsible god
who keeps popping the bubble
of romantic love
so our gated communion
swings open
to the greater community.

5. De-fickler

The sober god
who keeps fickle moods
from enslaving us:
derailing our integrity
commitments
and quality of service.

6. Tao-Devil

The introspective god
who helps us
see ourselves seeing
so we can cast out the devil
of personal reactivity
and surrender
to the Tao of each moment.

Weaving Headlights

All eyes, just weaving headlights.
One pilot: the unborn.
Lean drunken driver, lean
on this heart you call
"my horn."

911 Memorial

May this crude reenactment
of the tender demolition
we're all so heartsick for

drop our jaws
at the timeless presence
who is, even now,

riveted
by the YouTube disaster
that wears our name

and may we
bow down to the spot fires
erupting in the hallways

thanking them for driving us
floor by floor
onto the roof

so we can teeter
naked on the windy ledge
of each thought-murdering moment.

Bristlecone

Like a Bristlecone Pine
In a howling desert

may samsara design
a love strong and weathered.

Smoothie God

Hello, my name—my name is Awareness.
I'm in love with Myself.
I'd really love to love another Being
but there's no one else.

I turn the blade—the blade of silence—
deep in your smoothie mind.
I'm going to turn—turn your sorry science
into something divine.

I'm just a smoothie—
just a smoothie God.
And I'd like to turn your movie,
all your bitter fruity,
into Prasad.*

The things you call banana and mango
I call cradle and grave
I know it seems an unlikely combination
a drink for a slave.

*A devotional offering made to a god
typically consisting of food that is later shared among devotees.*

But if you come—you come a little closer
I'll give you a sip
of the bliss—the bliss of Mother Ocean
when she swallows your pit.

You see, I'm just a smoothie—
just a smoothie God.
And I'd like to turn your movie,
all your bitter fruity,
into Prasad.

I blend you with a little bit of sickness
and a dangerous lie.
Reach out the tongue—
the tongue of the witness.
Ah, It gets me so high.

A scoop of seeker, some disbeliever,
now add a rock in the road.
Just when it seems it couldn't get any bleaker:
oblivion alá mode!

I'm just a smoothie—
just a smoothie God.
And I'd like to turn your movie,
all your bitter fruity,
into Prasad.

This Storm

This storm needs a sky—
not an address.
A mom that stays home.

A window that stays bright
when all the fuses
of this body-mind are blown.

Traitor to the Sky

124 miles above us
extending, as best we know,
to eternity:
is a dark, soundless vacuum
whose temperatures hover between
233 and 454 degrees
below zero.

Meanwhile, down here,
a more temperate layer
of this mind-killing abyss
flushes through us like water
through the gills of a fish.

No wonder so many smiles
resemble a cringe.
When the dream turns solid
the soul flinches
and we feel like a traitor
to the sky that's hosting us.

Altar of Midnight

Pride
into petals

regrets
into incense

at the altar
of midnight
you turn all sins
into ceremony

Beloved Alchemist
I am yours

3

win yourself
back

Win Yourself Back

I am phenomenon in the eyes of a deeper seer.
I have won myself back.

All passing pleasures:
Finger food for the fullness of Being.

All clever word-craft:
Catalysts for silent communion.

Old hurts and defenses:
Hardened homesickness for You.

In the fire of pure seeing,
Self-worth scatters like ash in the wind.

All service:
Polishing the diamond of what is.

All relationship:
Mirrors for the enjoyment
of the Ageless One looking through.

All evil:
Evidence of a half-hearted detective.

All gossip:
Truth-tellers sprinting
towards the cliff edge of thought.

Better than ambition:
The calling that replaces me with You.

Better than activism:
The mutiny of timeless presence.

Better than sanctuary:
Standing tall for who we are—
in-your-face emptiness.

Happiness Class

At the end of this happiness class,
Professor Presence
will hand out
a simple, multiple choice quiz.

I am:

a) an entity
passing through experience.

b) an experience
passing through an entity.

Everyone passes,
but some
attend summer school
for eons.

Unexamined Riddle

Outward-facing
universe

why
do you exit
yourself?

Me-Goth

Remember when there were
solid, separate somebodies
instead of me-goth
inked into forever's forearm
and "falling for the trait bait"
was sexy fun?

Remember when cut flower psyches
had to wilt their way
into your heart
and conversations grew louder
than the dreamscape moaning
for a lucid dreamer?

Remember when activists
whipped frothy rapids
into the lazy river of time
and opinions were social lubricants
instead of thought activity
commenting on thought activity?

Now there are no people,
just tattoos asking why—

mythologies marching across
a skin-celled sky

cattle-brand charisma
with deep-space cry:
"person, sweet person—
die before you die."

Don't Ask-ness

Your toes, they need oasis:
a cool and shady sand.
Alas, Your resting places—
we call them faces—
our private brand.

Unmolested by the vastness
patriotic to half-mastness
Who am I?
Just call me
"Don't ask-ness."

Why Meditate?

Because every 12-hour flash
of our slow-strobing Sun
ignites a staggering masterpiece of animation:

primordial fuels
(fire, earth, air, water)
hissing as they feed a secret lantern—
consciousness incandescing
with or without us.

Because the silliest selfie
is a secret passageway
into an underground vault:

An Area 51
stacked high with forgotten archetypes—
kinesthetic codes
waiting to be meditatively cracked
so we can go face-to-face with

an intergalactic entity
whose been waiting aeons
for the incarnation, the day
the exact, obliterating instant

when we stop failing to feel
the loving vastness
looking out
of every pair of eyes.

12 Questions to Disappear In

1.

What watches
the impulse to act boldly?
Is presence
confident or unsure?

2.

What watches
the desire for secure ground?
Is presence
safe or vulnerable to ruin?

3.

What watches
the desire for change?
Is presence
bored or stimulated?

4.

What watches
the need to belong?
Is presence
cozy or orphaned?

5.

What watches
the impulse to perform?
Is presence
average or exceptional?

6.

What watches
the urge to improve?
Is presence
perfect or flawed?

7.

What watches
the impulse to peace-keep?
Is presence
polite or tactless?

8.

What watches
the desire to expose shadow?
Is presence
penetrating or superficial?

9.

What watches
ownership of belief?
Is presence
wise or simple-minded?

10.

What watches
the desire for success?
Is presence
competent or inept?

11.

What watches
the desire for community?
Is presence
a friend or a stranger?

12.

What watches
the urge to empathize?
Is presence
caring or clinical?

Persona Puppet

Look!

A persona-puppet
gone rogue

yanking
on its own jaw strings

cursing
the sky's dexterity

demanding
more, more, more

from its stiff
wooden nature.

Mystic Marriage Ceremony

Minister:
The honeymoon's over
new romance begins:
Sharing the center
of the wheel as it spins.

No marriage to save
or give up on.
We all need a grave
we can dance on.

Congregation:
I now pronounce you
awareness
in love
with itself.

Minister:
No world to land
on a somebody.
No bitter tea
in search of honey.

No mind that ends
in pure exhaustion.
We all need a chant
we can get lost in.

Congregation:
I now pronounce you
awareness
in love
with itself.

Minister:
Inspiring each other's
artistic absurdity.
Teasing beauty
from this world's insanity.

All the painful stories
of the past melt away.
The freshness of who we are
reborn everyday.

Congregation:
I now pronounce you
awareness
in love
with itself.

StarMonks

Half price at the airport
and first to board,
they drift
like blowing leaves
through the parking lot,
perfectly unmoved
by the Starbucks cups
flying from their sandals
like scurrying rats.

Their robes blend perfectly
with nothing—
papaya, maraschino—
succulent shades
designed to humiliate
our industrial-grey silence.
Straddling their rickety mopeds
putt-putting down inner alleyways
they engulf everyone in a cloud
of equanimity.

It's not hard to imagine,
if they lifted their gaze from the ground,
some of the things they might think:

Look over there—
a classic shot
of scenery's broken promise.

Have respect for the gentleman,
look away,
your mind, his mind—
tourists on the toilet
with the runs.

Over coffee, in my dreams,
I feel how— like a scalpel
around a suspicious freckle—
a grey-stubbled elder is tempted
to autopsy my gaze.

But no need.

He knows all about
the rolling Starbucks cups
proudly displaying
their broken lineage of heat
and why I refuse to study
the littered ground:

Too much like the ivory rats
to merge with them.

War Hero

You are a war hero.

How do I know?
You donned an Aries crash helmet
(the human skull),
scaled the barbed wire of gender,
got wounded by astrology's friendly fire
and somehow managed to infiltrate
the divine daydream.

Ever since then,
you can't stop jabbing your bayonet
at the wispy mosquito net
called "time."
How do I know?
The way you keep kicking at space
in the timeless trance
of your Pisces toes.

Yes, I know:
you're just a gentle soul on a stroll.

Call it what you will, dream-soldier,
I see what you are: a killing machine
forever pushing back
The Resistance to eternity-with-eyes.

How do I know?
How bravely you hand over your gait
to the off-world Author of footfalls.

Admit it:
You're more Rambo than Rumi.

Every day you stomp
through an inner killing field
littered with carnage far more gruesome
than severed limbs and crumpled corpses:
The relentless, blood-letting slaughter
of your peaceful self-image.
No power in heaven or earth
can stop you now.

How do I know?
Your presence is too smart
to grab at moods
dressed up as answers.

Brixton Saint

Drifting through the glassy gaze
of a diabetic sage,
orbs of unconditioned light:
the glow of devotion
twisting the fate
of a Jamaican art teacher
from Brixton.

Who is he?

The lion in my path—
a muscular luminosity
passing me by
on his way
to one of his own:
a baby cub
curled up and dying in the cage
of my self-concept.

With one clean swipe,
he maims me:

"As what are you speaking?"

Dumbstruck,
I answer with my life:

As your son, stung
by the desolation in the eyes
of a fellow cub
disguised as a grocery clerk
tethered
(like all of us)
to a rack of hellish bestsellers.

As your son, cheering on
the jittery orbs
scrambling for space
in the gaze of an adolescent Brixton saint
as mystery and memory
tussle for his tongue.

As your son, swooning
to the music
in your mystic growl:

"One kiss from god
and I walked out of my life."

Simmer

Like split pea and onion
dissolve into soup,
we simmer in silence,
you season, to suit.

How to Turn Clocks into Altars

Honor the mother-of-all time pieces
in your chest
prodding you to bow down
to the King of the beats.

Savor the space
between clock ticks:
refuge from an aging face
on a countdown.

Recognize repeated lateness
as aversion to incarnation—
a delusional shortcut to ascension
without having to hang
on the spirit/matter cross.

Choose transportive work
that keeps the dream
from turning solid
then call whatever shape
your life takes
"success."

Pause often to inquire:
Am I stepping soft
on the ground of undying presence
or am I time bound—
conterfeiting contentment
on a conveyor belt to death?

Then watch for the moment
when the seamless field of sentience
spreads like a shimmering mandala
all around you

and you stop mid-sentence
at a buzzy cafe
warmed by the fire
of eternal belonging.

21 Names for Awake

In-your-face
emptiness

Vastness
with a point of view

A wave
in love with ocean

Self-respecting
prostrator

Dream animal

Boundlessness
with a bark

Space
with a face

Nether-Brat

A sky
in puberty

Void-gasping
creature

Nameless eye-holes
bobbing to an addictive pulse

Oblivion
ala mode

Chatty savior

Bulk mail
from pure awareness

Identity-clouds drifting
through a sky of flesh

Crotch
of the Void

Sophisticated
psychological fairytale

Kicking mass of
"I don't knows"

Blip
with a lip

Sex stain
on God's bedspread

Crash helmet riding
on a timeless trance of toes

Dinner Mint

Dear dinner mint,
skin tight in foil of flesh,
I'm sorry—

no mentholated moment
alone with you
could ever match

the tiramisu
equanimity is serving.

Acknowledgments

THIS BOOK, and virtually all of my success as a teacher, writer and counselor, would not have been possible without the skilled guidance and loving support of my beloved partner, Jane Brunette.

I would also like to extend a deep bow of gratitude to the many students and clients who have, over the years, opened their innermost hearts to me. It is your vulnerable revealing that has pushed me to poetically name the archetypal longings of the soul.

Most of all, I give thanks for the grace of my beloved teacher, Mooji. These poems were ignited by the steady flame of his devotion. His ego-dissolving presence keeps pushing me to string together the kind of thoughts that might take us to the cliff edge of thought.

About the Author

HUNTER REYNOLDS was born in Chicago and raised in an intentional community based on the teachings of 17th-century mystic Emmanuel Swedenborg. He has since been deeply influenced by Advaita, Buddhism and the non-dual teachings of Mooji.

In his work as a professional astrologer, Hunter weaves non-dual wisdom with the body/mind insights of astrology, creating a unique form of counseling called "Astrodharma" in which the astrological archetypes are understood as styles of awakening.

Hunter travels widely, speaking with clients from all over the world. He welcomes your feedback and comments on this book. His websites are astrodharma.org and bravenewprayers.com.

About Flamingseed Press

FLAMINGSEED PRESS is a boundary-crossing experiment in publishing. The mission: To publish books that grapple with the challenge of marrying spirit to earth. They cross boundaries of culture and religion, genre and paradigm, all with the intention of taking fast-changing times and challenging circumstances as inspiration to find more wise and soulful ways to live on our endangered planet, cultivating connection rather than division, love rather than fear.

In addition to *Fukishima Fortune Cookies,* the press has thus far published two other volumes of mystic poetry: *Brave New Prayers* by Hunter Reynolds and *Grasshopper Guru* by Jane Brunette. A series of books on soul practices are currently under development. Visit flamingseedpress.com.

flamingseed
press

Imagine Rumi Raised on YouTube.

Not to mention global warming and all the trappings of racy western culture.
What brave new metaphors might he draw upon to convey his "astounding, lucid, confusion?"

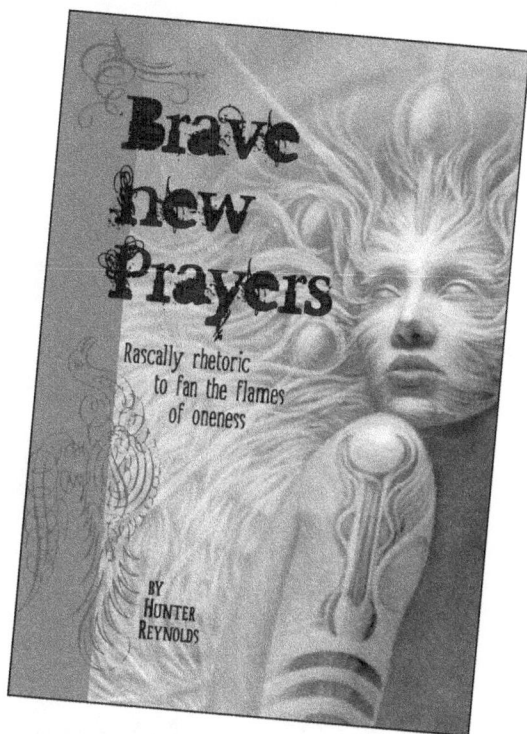

Brave New Prayers
BY HUNTER REYNOLDS
available through your local bookstore or amazon.com

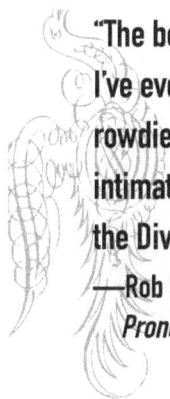

"The best prayer book I've ever found—the holiest, rowdiest, truest and most intimately connected with the Divine Wow."
—Rob Brezsny, author of *Pronoia is the Antidote for Paranoia*

flamingseedpress.com

How to Pray:

Hide under a blanket with the real and tell everything. Empty your insides. Say out loud those damp things in the shadows. Dry them in the sun——then decide what to keep.

12 Wheels of Karma

Astrology as a tool of meditation & self-inquiry

BY HUNTER REYNOLDS

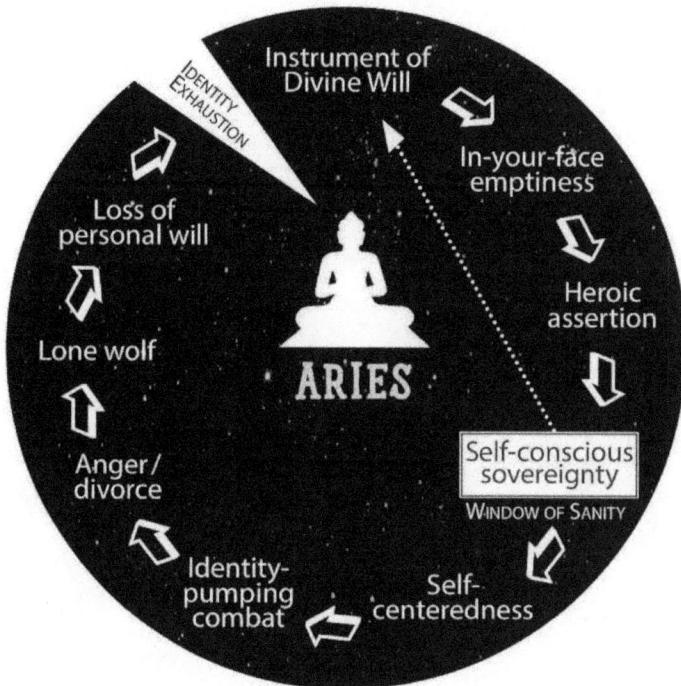

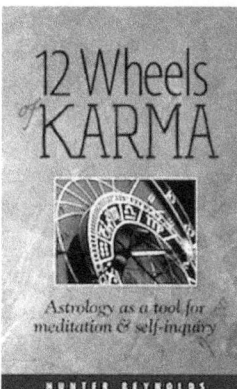

Instrument of
Divine Will

IDENTITY
EXHAUSTION

In-your-face
emptiness

Loss of
personal will

Heroic
assertion

Lone wolf

ARIES

Anger/
divorce

Self-conscious
sovereignty

WINDOW OF SANITY

Identity-
pumping
combat

Self-
centeredness

12 Wheels
of KARMA
Astrology as a tool for
meditation & self-inquiry
HUNTER REYNOLDS

www.ingramcontent.com/pod-product-compliance
Lightning Source LLC
LaVergne TN
LVHW091227080426
835509LV00009B/1203